BUILT WITH PRIDE

Tyne ships: 1969-1994

*This book is dedicated to the best shipbuilders:
the men and women of Swan Hunter.*

by

Ken Smith and Ian Rae

Published by Newcastle upon Tyne City Libraries & Arts

Front cover:

Last ship of a long line. The frigate HMS *Richmond* leaves Wallsend on November 3 1994 for her delivery voyage.

(Photo: Gavin Duthie)

Back cover:

Daughter of the Tyne. The Type 23 Duke Class frigate HMS *Richmond* on the building berth at the Wallsend shipyard.

(Photo: Swan Hunter staff photographer)

Acknowledgements:

Ian Stokoe, Price Waterhouse.
Tyne and Wear Archives, Tyne and Wear PTE.
Norman Gilchrist, Ed Jackson, Jan Lowry, Gavin Duthie.
The authors also wish to thank Pat Cook for her work in preparing the manuscript.

© Ken Smith and Ian Rae, 1995.
© City of Newcastle upon Tyne , Community and Leisure Services Department, Libraries & Arts, 1995.
Photographs © Swan Hunter Shipbuilders / Tyne and Wear Archives, unless otherwise indicated.

Swan Hunter photographs were taken by staff photographers Stan Forster, Derek Harris and Gavin Duthie.

British Library Cataloguing-in-Publication Data.
A catalogue record for this book is available from the British Library.

ISBN: 1 85795 091 7

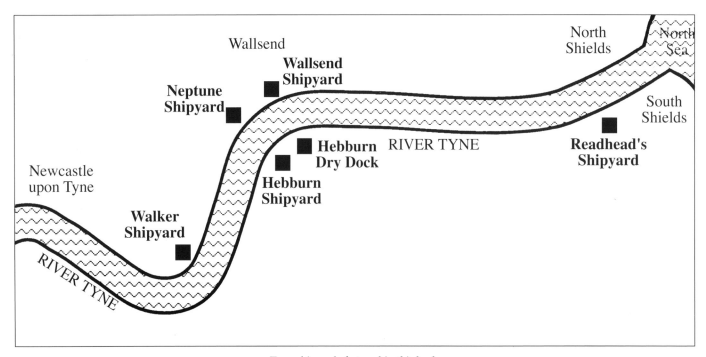

Tyne shipyards featured in this book.

INTRODUCTION

In May 1993 the world renowned Tyne shipbuilder Swan Hunter called in the receivers after failing to win a vital order for the helicopter carrier HMS *Ocean*. The last shipbuilding company left on a river which had produced so many great ships was plunged into an unprecedented crisis.

During the next 18 months nearly all Swan's 2,200 workers lost their jobs. On 3 November 1994 what looked to many like being the Tyne's last ship, the Type 23 frigate HMS *Richmond*, left the Wallsend yard for delivery to the Royal Navy. There were no more orders and the fitting-out quays and building berths were empty.

The receivers disposed of Swan Hunter's Neptune yard and Hebburn Dry Dock to ship repair companies. The Wallsend yard was advertised for sale worldwide.

Few could have envisaged this social and industrial tragedy in the years 1966-1968 when Swan Hunter merged with other shipyards on the Tyne, including those of Readhead and Sons at South Shields, Vickers Armstrong at Walker and Hawthorn Leslie at Hebburn. The group was further expanded in late 1968 by the addition of the Furness Shipbuilding Company's Haverton Hill yard at Stockton-on-Tees. Also included in this 'consortium' was Smiths Dock of South Bank, Middlesbrough, and Cleland's yard at Willington Quay on the Tyne.

Swan Hunter remained the dominant partner in this large grouping of shipyards under one company.

In 1977 the company was nationalised, but nearly nine years later reverted to private ownership as a result of a management buy-out. Teesside's Smiths Dock and Haverton Hill yard left the group after nationalisation. By 1989 Wallsend was the only yard on the Tyne still launching ships. However, ship repairing and refitting continued at other sites along its banks.

Many fine vessels were constructed on Tyneside in the years 1969 to 1994 which showed the workforce to be the equal of any in the world at producing ships of high quality. This book surveys much of the output of those years. They were ships built with pride.

This ethos of pride in a job well done which the workers of the Tyne possess has been passed on from generation to generation. At the Swan Hunter yards it was intermingled with a feeling that everyone was part of a large family, a family which had its disagreements and differences at times, but which was nevertheless held together by the warmth of friendship and good humour as well as the common interest of earning a living.

Dick Gonsalez, the leader of the Confederation of Shipbuilding and Engineering Unions at the Wallsend yard and treasurer of Wallsend AEEU, worked in the yards for 33 years before being made redundant. He is a marine plumber and pipework welder.

Dick accused the Government of operating the "economics of the madhouse" because the cost of social security payments, redundancy payments and other financial outlays would far outweigh the cost of keeping the shipyard open and people in jobs. He believed the Government had been motivated by political considerations in failing to support Swan's.

"I am very bitter," he said, pointing to the plight of young families with large mortgages who had been particularly badly hit by the redundancies.

He stressed that the apprenticeship schemes at Swan's had acted as a skills base for industry throughout the North East. Shipbuilding was a high-skills industry and many companies had benefited from the workers trained in the yards.

Commenting on the collapse of the company, he said: "Every time I speak about the subject I get a lump in my throat. Swan's was a community inside a community. It was like a big family. The job losses were a major funeral as far as we were concerned."

Mick Bonham, a designer in the naval architects' department at Wallsend with 12 years experience at Swan's, was one of the last to be made redundant.

"What has happened to the company is a disgrace. It needn't have happened. The two years of receivership have been fraught with uncertainty. You can't plan your life. I'm saddened for others more than myself. I've been one of the lucky ones in being among the last to leave."

Mick added: "Shipbuilding is team work. Each person and department is part of a chain aimed at producing a vessel. Each member of the workforce, from a manager downwards, is of equal importance."

The significance of team work was confirmed by Norman Gilchrist. He worked at Swan's for 42 years, starting as a shipwright and rising to become production director. He was also chief draughtsman for many years. Norman's final job before retirement was as project director for the aircraft carrier *Ark Royal*. "She was a happy ship," he recalled. Other favourite vessels of his included the Norwegian Liner *Bergensfjord*, the Tyne-Norway ferry *Leda* and the unique destroyer HMS *Bristol*.

"Swan's was a splendid place to work," he said. "It was my life. I am terribly sorry the younger people will not now be able to have the experience I had."

Of the team work in the yards, he said: "If you were a manager you were no better than the men who worked under you. You were dependent on their quality. We all wanted to make a good job of building a ship. You had to. If you didn't there was always the worry that the shipowner might not come back to place other orders."

Jan Lowry, a telephone operator with Swan's for 21 years, said: "I have thoroughly enjoyed being part of a team which could produce any sort of vessel on any kind of scale to the highest standards of technology. I am very angry. The collapse of the company is a tragic waste of skilled manpower and facilities. It's so short-sighted because we are an island nation."

Jan's husband, Bob, a joiner, worked at the Swan Hunter yards for 22 years. "The hardship caused and the interference in family life for so many ex-workers is tragic," he said.

Bob pointed out that no money had been made available to keep a first rate workforce and company together, who had done their utmost to assist the defence of the country over many years.

"The Swan Hunter workforce produced and delivered on time the last three frigates to the highest standards. Under the uncertain conditions imposed by receivership this proved their skill, pride and dignity beyond doubt."

Bob said he missed the shipyard humour and camaraderie. He would never forget the pride felt by them all on delivery of a new ship.

Gavin Duthie, who was one of the three Swan's photographers, said: "It is a terrible waste. There has been no political will to keep the yard alive … There is this misconception that shipbuilding is some sort of outdated, smoke-stack industry. But it isn't. Swan's was at the forefront of technology."

Ken Moreland, who worked at Swan's as a stager (scaffolder) for 21 years before being made redundant in 1994, said: "I enjoyed going to work. You had a bit of fun and laughter. The redundancies were terrible. You arrived every morning and thought: 'Is it going to be my turn?' You saw mates you might have worked with for 20 years told they had to go. I saw some good lads go. I've seen some cry."

Lee Binney, a caulker for 10 years who was involved in the job of making sure ships were watertight, said: "To see your friends get paid off was the worst thing. I felt so guilty. When I was eventually paid off it was like a weight off my shoulders. The Government had the opportunity on numerous occasions to bail Swan's out but they didn't. You couldn't fault the unions. They did all they could to keep the shipyard open. If the Government had put as much effort into saving Swan's as the unions did it wouldn't have collapsed. There was never any industrial action and the workers just got on with their jobs."

Terry Summerson served his time as an apprentice draughtsman between 1965 and 1970 and later became a production engineer. "The collapse of Swan's is a major loss to this country of shipbuilding skills and capability," he said.

Terry, who was in the first wave of employees to be made redundant, said that many technical workers who had now found jobs had to live away from home during the working week and travel back to Tyneside at weekends. They were generally on short-term contracts.

Norman Lancaster worked for the company in various capacities for a total of 14 years. He was a sheet metal worker, then a production engineer and finally a draughtsman before he too lost his job in the first batch of redundancies at the end of May 1993. His wife had given birth to a baby boy only weeks earlier.

"It was like a bad fairy tale," he said. "You couldn't grasp the reality of it. When you were made redundant you thought, 'Is this really happening?'"

Norman commented: "Swan's ships went out from the Tyne with zero defects. They built the best vessels in the fleet. The Navy said we had done a great job."

This last point is perhaps one of the most telling. Swan's had a reputation for top-quality shipbuilding in the Royal Navy. Quality was also matched by unstinting effort. In 1982 the workforce completed the aircraft carrier HMS *Illustrious* 12 weeks ahead of schedule so that she could be sent to the Falklands as soon as possible. This early completion of a major vessel was a prodigious feat by the workforce.

Given the company's fine track record, the question that must be asked is: Why did the Government fail to support Swan's in its hour of greatest need?

Ken Smith, May 1995

CONTENTS

*All photographs are from the collection of Swan Hunter Shipbuilders -
Tyne and Wear Archives, unless otherwise indicated. Where possible
the photographer is acknowledged.*

*Crane's-eye view. **Esso Hibernia** leaves the Tyne. This picture was taken from the hammerhead crane of the Wallsend Slipway and Engineering Company.*

Esso Hibernia

(Yard No. 4, Wallsend, completed 1970). The second of eight supertankers built at Wallsend between 1968 and 1976. Like her sister, *Esso Northumbria*, the *Esso Hibernia* cost £6.5 million to build. Over 30,000 tons of steel were used in her construction.

Her 250,000 tonnes of oil were carried at 15 knots. For a short time in 1982 *Esso Hibernia* was used as a static oil storage vessel. The following year she was broken up in Taiwan, a fate shared by her sister.

*An impressive view of the supertanker **Texaco Great Britain**.*
Demand for building berths delayed her construction.

Texaco Great Britain

(Yard No. 5, Wallsend, completed 1971). Ordered in 1967, this supertanker was not completed until four years later because the great demand for building berths delayed her construction. She put in sterling service until November 1980 when she arrived at Dakar in West Africa with severe hull damage, which had been suffered on a voyage from Port Arthur in the Far East. Because of the economic problems in the oil trade at the time the repairs were considered too costly and she was towed to Taiwan for breaking up.

*The replenishment tanker **Green Rover** on trials in the North Sea*

Green Rover

(Yard No. 6, Hebburn, completed 1969). This small Royal Fleet Auxiliary tanker was one of three sisters launched at Hebburn. Their purpose was to follow and supply fuel, fresh water and dry stores to Royal Navy warships during worldwide operations. The Rover tankers were built to carry about 6,800 tons of cargo at a speed of 15 knots. A large flight deck was fitted aft for Sea King helicopters.

In 1985 *Green Rover* was in mid-Atlantic when Richard Branson's *Virgin Challenger* boat ran out of fuel while attempting to gain the record for the fastest crossing. The ship was able to give *Virgin Challenger* fuel to continue. *Green Rover* was sold in 1992 to the Indonesian government, refitted at the Neptune Yard in Low Walker, and renamed *Kri Arun*. She is still in service.

Sisters take shape.
Atlantic Causeway *and*
Atlantic Conveyor *under*
construction at Walker in 1969

Atlantic Causeway and *Atlantic Conveyor*

(Yard Nos. 1, 2 Walker, completed 1969, 1970). Laid down in April 1968, *Atlantic Causeway* was built for Cunard as their contribution to the European shipping consortium Atlantic Container Lines. This ship, along with her sister *Atlantic Conveyor*, was built to carry 870 containers and almost 1,000 vehicles across the Atlantic on fast passage at more than 24 knots. Requisitioned during the Falklands War, she was fitted with a 'ski' ramp for Harrier jet operations. Afterwards, *Atlantic Causeway* was laid up in Liverpool. She was broken up in Taiwan in 1986. Like her sister, *Atlantic Conveyor* was also requisitioned for service in the Falklands conflict. On 25 May 1982 she was hit by an Exocet missile fired by an Argentine aircraft. It had been aimed at a warship in the Task Force but was deflected by anti-missile chaff and struck the container ship. *Atlantic Conveyor* sank six days later. The ship's captain and 11 of the crew lost their lives. A second vessel named *Atlantic Conveyor* was completed at the Wallsend yard in early 1985.

*Mexican workhorse **Emiliano Zapata** goes through her paces in North Sea trials.*

Emiliano Zapata

(Yard No. 11, Hebburn, completed 1970). The Hebburn Yard became the Tyne's specialist in building liquefied gas carriers. These gases are carried at very low temperatures. The *Emiliano* *Zapata* was built for the state-owned Mexican oil company Pemex. She runs on a shuttle service up and down the Mexican coast. The ship was named after a famous Mexican revolutionary leader.

*Container ship **Dart Atlantic** on trials in May 1971.*

Dart Atlantic

(Yard No. 15, Walker, completed 1971). This container ship joined her sister, *Dart America*, on the transatlantic run in May 1971. She was later sold to Far East owner CY Tung.

The vessel was renamed *CP Ambassador* in 1981 and five years later became *Canmar Ambassador*.

Dunstanburgh Castle leaves the Wallsend Shipyard after visiting the Tyne to pick up stores prior to trials. The stern of a supertanker can be seen top left.

Dunstanburgh Castle

(Yard No. 18, Furness, completed 1970). Constructed for shipowners Souter's of Newcastle, the *Dunstanburgh Castle* could carry over 100,000 tonnes of bulk cargo such as grain or coal. In July 1981 she ran aground while on passage from Vancouver to Korea. Further damage was suffered by a fire and explosion in her engine room. However, the ship was repaired and then sold to South Korean owners who renamed her *Global Hope*. She traded worldwide until broken up in India in 1994.

Merkara, one of four cargo ships ordered by the British India Line in 1968. All were built at the Neptune yard.

Merkara

(Yard No. 22, Neptune, completed 1971). One of four cargo ships ordered by the British India Line in 1968, like her sisters, *Merkara* cost about £2.75 million to build. Her career mirrored those of her sisters, the ship being transferred to P & O's general cargo division and renamed *Strathmay* in 1975. After her sale to the United Thai Shipping Corporation she became *Kannikar*. The vessel was broken up in China in 1987.

Ian Rae

World Unicorn

*Gigantic neighbour. The supertanker **World Unicorn** towers above a Wallsend street.*

(Yard No. 28, Wallsend, completed 1974). Princess Anne launched the Tyne's first supertanker, *Esso Northumbria*, in 1969 and three years later, on 3 May 1972, she returned to the Wallsend Yard to launch another, the *World Unicorn*. This ship was built for the Hong Kong World Wide Shipping Co.

By 1979 she was laid up and being used as an oil storage vessel for kerosene and diesel oil in Sumatra, Indonesia. She acted as a distribution point for trans-shipping her cargo to other vessels for delivery to Indonesian islands. *World Unicorn* was broken up in Taiwan in 1984.

The Strick Line's final ship. **Nigaristan** *leaving the Tyne, taken from the Groyne, South Shields.*

Nigaristan

(Yard No. 32, Readhead's, completed 1970). This was the last ship to be built for the Strick Line, whose distinctive funnel colours had been almost a landmark in South Shields since the Second World War.

Launched in June 1970, *Nigaristan* was transferred within the P & O Group and renamed *Strathaird*. She was sold to Greek owners in 1979 and they operated her for seven years. The ship was broken up in China.

Shipyard artist Lewis W. Thomson ('Alfie')

*Graceful queen. An artist's impression of the New Zealand passenger ferry **Rangatira** in service. The picture was drawn by Lewis W. Thomson ('Alfie') whose artistic and interpretive skills helped persuade many an owner to 'build Swans'.*

Rangatira

(Yard No. 33, Walker, completed 1972). This New Zealand ferry was built to link Wellington in the country's North Island with Lyttelton near Christchurch in South Island. She replaced the *Wahine* which had been tragically lost in 1968. Completed in 1972, *Rangatira* had accommodation for 1,600 passengers and vehicles. However, she proved to be a loss-making ship as many New Zealanders switched to aircraft for the journey and she was plagued by engine problems. *Rangatira* was withdrawn from service and offered for sale.

By the late 1970s she was being used as an accommodation vessel for oil rig workers on the Scottish coast and at the Sullom Voe oil terminal in the Shetlands. During the Falklands War *Rangatira* served as a troopship. She did not arrive back in Britain until the autumn of 1983 when she was given a refit and laid up. In 1987 she was sold to Cypriot owners for service in the Mediterranean, being renamed the *Queen M*. In 1990 the vessel was sold again, this time to Italian owners. She currently sails under the name of *Carlo R*.

*A ship is born. **Chemical Explorer** is launched from the Hebburn yard in 1971. Supertanker **London Lion**, at Wallsend, is in the background on her berth.*

Chemical Explorer

(Yard No. 36, Hebburn, completed 1972). This chemical tanker was built for the Anglo Norness Group and ran trials in April 1972. She plied her trade between the USA and European ports. In 1982 she was chartered out to the Ministry of Defence in a support role to the Task Force following the end of the Falklands conflict. Bought by Cypriot owners in 1985, the ship was renamed *Brilliant*. She later acted as a shuttle tanker along the West African coast.

Neptune's elegant daughter. **Vistafjord** *on trials in 1972.*

Vistafjord

(Yard No. 39, Neptune, completed 1973). The last passenger liner to be built on the Tyne, this ship is today one of Cunard's most prestigious cruise liners. She was originally constructed for the Norwegian America Line's transatlantic route and for worldwide cruising. In 1983 she was sold, along with her sister *Sagafjord*, to Cunard who were expanding their cruising operations and wanted "simply the best ships available". *Vistafjord* has a gross tonnage of 24,492 and is 629 ft long. Launched on 15 May 1972, she was delivered to her first owners in Norway a year later. Driven by diesel engines linked to twin screws, she can cruise at more than 20 knots with a maximum speed of nearly 23 knots. She has ice-strengthened bows as a precaution for the trips to the North Cape of Norway and Spitzbergen. Other features include two 15 ft long stabilisers. The ship has taken passengers on holidays to almost every corner of the world, favourite areas including the Caribbean, Mediterranean, Black Sea, Canary Islands and Scandinavia.

*The cargo ship **Corabank** which was launched at the Readhead's yard, South Shields.*

Corabank

(Yard No. 49, Readhead's, completed 1973). In May 1970 Swan Hunter received an order for six cargo ships to be built for the Bank Line's round-the-world service on an 18-week cycle. Most of the ports of call are in the Pacific, including Fiji, New Guinea and Tahiti. The ships were designed with a small amount of passenger accommodation.

Like her sisters, *Corabank* could carry 15,500 tonnes of cargo at a service speed of 18 knots. In her first four years of service she covered over 300,000 miles. In 1984 *Corabank* was sold to Peruvian owners and in 1988 to owners in Singapore. Her career lasted another five years before she was scrapped in India.

*Courtesy visit. HMS **Newcastle** returns to the Tyne in 1984.*

HMS *Newcastle*

(Yard No. 61, Neptune, completed 1978). HMS *Newcastle* was the first of a new breed of guided missile destroyers to be built at the yard. Known as Type 42 destroyers, they were designed to be the 'eyes' of the fleet, acting as long-range pickets for the air defence of a task force. In July 1988 *Newcastle* was damaged in a freak accident when on trials off Portsmouth. Her radar guided Phalanx gun accidentally hit the towing wire of an aluminium tube being pulled by a fighter aircraft simulating a missile attack. The tube was deflected and entered the starboard engine intake, causing damage to the engine room. The ship has visited most parts of the world and is now nearing the end of her service life with the Royal Navy.

The river's largest ship. **Tyne Pride** *passes the Collingwood Monument at Tynemouth in 1976.*

Tyne Pride

(Yard No. 63, Wallsend, completed 1976). This supertanker was built as part of a venture by Swan Maritime, a joint company in which the builders had a stake. The plan was to sell various types of tankers to a perceived market. Although launched as the *Tyne Pride*, the ship never traded under this name.

She was sold to Liberians who renamed her *Opportunity*. Later she sailed under the French flag as the *Thermidor* for 10 years. She currently runs on the world's oil routes as the *New Resource*. At 262,000 deadweight tonnes, she is the largest ship ever built on the Tyne.

Built in two yards. **Yorkshire**, *from the Walker yard looking down river.*

Yorkshire

(Yard No. 65, Hebburn Dock and Walker, completed 1975). This medium-sized tanker of 112,000 deadweight tonnes was sold to the Bibby Line of Liverpool while under construction. The aft end of the ship was built and launched at Walker and the fore section at the Hebburn Dock complex. The two sections were then joined together. In 1985 *Yorkshire* was chartered out for six years as a storage tanker in the Persian Gulf, taking the name *York Marine*. However, in April 1988 the ship was attacked by Iranian gunboats and a blaze broke out aboard. Abandoned for a short time, she was later repaired and resumed her storage role. In 1989 Cypriot owners returned her to active oil trading. The vessel was broken up in India in 1993.

*One of five sisters, a **Robkap** class tanker passes North Shields.*

The Robkap Tankers

(Yard Nos. 69 to 73, Hebburn and Neptune, completed 1975-1976). Between 1973 and 1976 five oil products tankers of 30,000 deadweight tonnes were built for Nikreis Maritime. Upon completion they all took the names of former Russian fleet oil ships. Suspicions were raised at the time that they too would be used in the same role to supply the Soviet Navy with fuel.

However, the ships are still trading today as normal tankers for various companies with Russian interests. They carry the names *Maykop, Asheron, Grozny, Godermes* and *Makhachkala*. The names by which they were originally known while under construction were *Helena 'K', Robkap II, Robkap I, Robkap IV* and *Robkap III* respectively.

Awarded battle honours in the Gulf War. The Neptune-built Type 42 destroyer HMS **Exeter**.

HMS *Exeter*

Exeter (Yard No. 101, Neptune, completed 1980). This Type 42 destroyer was delivered to the Royal Navy in August 1980 and was soon hard at work. In 1982 she was guardship in Belize when the Falklands War broke out and was sent south to the conflict to replace two sister ships which had been lost, HMS *Sheffield* and HMS *Coventry*. She did a second spell of duty in the Falklands after the war ended.

In 1985 *Exeter* was deployed to the Persian Gulf and the Indian Ocean, taking part in two rescue missions for missing ships. In 1991 the destroyer was in the thick of it once more during the Gulf War for which she was awarded battle honours. More recently, she has served with *Ark Royal*'s task force in the Adriatic enforcing the UN embargoes. *Exeter* is still in service.

*Delivered ahead of schedule, HMS **Illustrious** leaving the Tyne on her delivery voyage in 1982.*

HMS *Illustrious*

(Yard No. 102, Wallsend, completed 1982). This ship was the first aircraft carrier to be built at the yard for over 20 years. Ordered in April 1976, *Illustrious* was launched into the Tyne by Princess Margaret on 1 December 1978. The vessel was then moved up river to the Walker yard for fitting out. As relations with the Argentinians deteriorated in the spring of 1982, the Royal Navy requested that her completion be speeded up. The workforce responded magnificently and the result was that this highly complex modern aircraft carrier was completed 12 weeks ahead of schedule. The ship sailed from the Tyne on 18 June 1982 with crowds lining the banks of the river to bid her farewell. *Illustrious* joined the second wave of ships assigned to the Falklands task force, returning to Britain for Christmas 1982. The next year there were some red faces amongst the ship's company and Ministry of Defence when one of her Harriers ran out of fuel during operations off the Portuguese coast. The crew of a passing coaster were amazed when the pilot landed his aircraft on the ship's hatch covers! *Illustrious* led a Royal Navy task force around the world showing the flag in 1986. The carrier was sent for a long and intensive refit at Devonport in August 1991. She emerged in time to act as flagship for the D-Day anniversary Spithead Naval Review in June 1994.

On the stocks. **Starman Anglia** *under construction at the Neptune Yard.*

Starman Anglia

(Yard No. 1337, Neptune, completed 1984). A roll on/roll off heavy lift ship, *Starman Anglia* was designed to operate as a multi-purpose heavy cargo carrier worldwide. She was fitted with a 300-tonne capacity derrick. Only the hull was built at Neptune. After the launch the ship was towed to Smiths Dock (another part of the group) on the Tees for fitting out. In 1984 she was sold to Yugoslav owners.

Pacific Teal, *one of four nuclear waste carriers constructed at Hebburn Dock and the Hebburn yard.*

Pacific Teal

(Yard Nos. 106 Hebburn Shipyard, 110, 115 and 116, Hebburn Dock, completed 1979-82). *Pacific Swan*, *Pacific Crane*, *Mediterranean Shearwater* and *Pacific Teal* were built to carry nuclear waste in large concrete and steel containers from Japan and Europe to the Sellafield reprocessing plant in Cumbria.

In 1992 *Pacific Crane*, which had been temporarily transferred to the Japanese flag for one voyage, had her cargo crane removed and hatches sealed to prevent any possible terrorist interception while on a voyage to France with an armed escort.

Kopalnia Gottwald

(Yard No. 108, Hebburn Dock, completed 1980). This ship was built as a result of efforts by a Labour government in the 1970s to keep Britain's yards going during a period when there were few orders. The government struck a deal with the state-owned Polish Ocean Lines for a series of vessels to be constructed under joint ownership. *Kopalnia Gottwald* was the only one to be built on the Tyne. A 17,000 deadweight tonnes bulk carrier, she traded from Poland exporting the country's coal. In 1993 the ship was sold to a company in the Marshall Islands of the Pacific and renamed *Jamno*.

Polish bulk carrier. **Kopalnia Gottwald** *being floated out of Hebburn Dock.*

*Giant on the berth. **Ark Royal** under construction at the Wallsend Shipyard in 1980.*

HMS *Ark Royal*

(Yard No. 109, Wallsend, completed 1985). The flagship of the Royal Navy, this modern aircraft carrier is one of the most important ships to be built on the Tyne. Launched by the Queen Mother on 2 June 1981, the *Ark*, as she is affectionately known, is the fifth Royal Navy ship to bear this proud name since 1588. The vessel was fitted out at the Walker yard. Like many other warships, she is powered by gas turbine engines and her aircraft include the Sea Harrier. Prominent features are her 'ski' ramp and two huge funnels. Her career to date has covered many operations throughout the world. In October 1988 she was the flagship of the Fleet Review at Sydney for the Australian bicentennial celebrations. In 1994 she completed her second spell of duty in the Adriatic Sea off the former Yugoslavian coast. Afterwards, the *Ark* paid a courtesy visit to the Tyne, the river of her birth, before beginning a major refit.

The Hebburn Dock oil tanker **BP Achiever**. *As* **Australian Achiever** *she trades along the Australian coast and to Singapore.*

BP Achiever

(Yard No. 112, Hebburn Dock, completed 1983). A tanker with a carrying capacity of 127,000 tonnes of oil, *BP Achiever* was built for the Australian coastal trade and also operates on a shuttle service to Singapore with refined oil. In 1991 she was renamed *Australian Achiever*. She was the first of a new breed of vessel to be built in the UK, being designated a segregated ballast tanker.

*The versatile cargo ship **Hoegh Duke**. She was constructed for a round-the-world service.*

Hoegh Duke

(Yard No. 118, Wallsend, completed 1984). A large cargo ship designed to carry a wide range of goods, including lumber, containers, cars and coal, she was built for a round-the-world service along with three Finnish sister ships. *Hoegh Duke* is owned like many ships today by a 'bank' which leases her out to operators. Her profile is dominated by large cargo handling equipment.

*The diving support vessel **Orelia**. Only the steel hull was built at Neptune. She was fitted out on the Humber.*

Derek Ampleford

Orelia

(Yard No. 120, Neptune, completed 1982). *Orelia* is a diving support vessel built for Houlder Brothers' operations in the North Sea. Only the steel hull was built at Neptune and she was fitted out on the Humber. The ship has accommodation for 100 and is equipped with two special diving pools for seabed operations. In 1989 she was taken over by the Stena group and now operates as the *Stena Orelia*.

*Neptune cableship. **Pacific Guardian** returns to the Tyne after trials.*

Pacific Guardian

(Yard No. 122, Neptune, completed 1984). From the turn of the century cable laying and repairing ships were always a speciality of the Neptune yard, two dozen coming from its slipways. Nine of these ships saw service with Cable & Wireless. After a gap of some years these owners returned to the Tyne to order *Pacific Guardian*. She was designed to be based in Fiji as a cable repair ship for the telephone link between Australia and western Canada. The *Sir Eric Sharp*, the only cableship to be built at Wallsend (Yard No. 128, 1989), has a similar role maintaining Atlantic cables.

*HMS **Sheffield** works up to full speed on trials off the Northumberland coast.*

HMS *Sheffield*

(Yard No. 123, Neptune, completed 1988). Following the tragic loss of ships in the Falklands War of 1982, it was decided to replace the vessels with larger ships but to retain the names of those sunk. HMS *Sheffield* and her sister HMS *Coventry* were ordered in December 1982 and commissioned six years later. *Sheffield* has completed two tours of duty with the Armilla Patrol in the Persian Gulf. During the Gulf War she kept station in the eastern Mediterranean with the *Ark Royal* task group. In December 1991 the ship attended the 50th anniversary remembrance events to mark the sinking of the *Repulse* and *Prince of Wales* off the coast of Malaya during the Second World War.

*Launched in darkness. HMS **Coventry** on trials.*

HMS *Coventry*

(Yard No. 124, Wallsend, completed 1988). This ship was launched during the hours of darkness in the early morning of 8 April 1986. An industrial dispute had threatened to delay the launch for three months until there was another suitable tide. *Coventry* has been mainly deployed in protecting the shipping lanes of the Persian Gulf. However, life is not all work with the Royal Navy. For example, in October 1992 she took part, along with HMS *Cardiff*, in a 'jolly' to Nassau in the Bahamas for the Columbus celebrations.

*Wallsend knight. The new RFA **Sir Galahad**, a landing ship, alongside at Wallsend.*

RFA *Sir Galahad*

(Yard No. 125, Wallsend, completed 1988). This landing ship was built to replace her namesake which was attacked with tragic consequences at Bluff Cove during the Falklands War of 1982. At the launch a detachment of Welsh Guards were in attendance to pay their respects to the new ship. The replacement is a larger vessel capable of carrying 339 soldiers and their vehicles. *Sir Galahad* has been involved in several amphibious exercises with the Royal Marines in Norway. During the Gulf War she acted as a support ship for the United Nations minesweeping squadron and for this role she was awarded battle honours.

*Last ship launched at Neptune. HMS **Chatham** leaves the Tyne for delivery.*

HMS *Chatham*

(Yard No. 126, Neptune, completed 1989). *Chatham* was the last ship to be launched at the Neptune yard. She entered the Tyne in January 1988. Although designated a frigate, she is the size of a Second World War cruiser. In 1991 the ship was attached to NATO's standing naval force in the Atlantic. Later she was deployed to the Gulf.

RFA *Fort George*

(Yard No. 129, Wallsend, completed 1993). A large multi-purpose replenishment ship built to supply Royal Navy vessels on deployments worldwide. The *Fort George* carries oil, food, ammunition and many other stores. It was originally planned that six of these giant vessels would be built, but in the end *Fort George* was the second and last of the class. Her sister ship is *Fort Victoria*. It was also planned that she would carry a vertical Seawolf missile silo for protection against air attack, but the idea has not been implemented. The concept of launching missiles from an oil tanker when hazardous oil vapours are present must have given the crew nightmares!

*Ship in the night, RFA **Fort George** on the building berth at Wallsend prior to launch.*

*Icebreaker from Wallsend. The **James Clark Ross** passes the Collingwood Monument as she returns to the Tyne from trials.*

RRS *James Clark Ross*

(Yard No. 132, Wallsend, completed 1991). Launched by the Queen, this Royal Research Ship was built for the National Environment Research Council and is operated by the British Antarctic Survey. The *James Clark Ross* serves five research stations in the Antarctic and also carries out projects researching into the seas and the Earth's core. She is equipped with powerful diesel engines, giving her the necessary force to break ice. The ship was the first to be launched from the yard by a reigning monarch.

*Submarine hunter. The Type 23 frigate HMS **Westminster** in the Tyne.*

HMS *Westminster*, HMS *Northumberland*, HMS *Richmond*

(Yard Nos. 135 completed 1993, 136 completed 1994, and 137 completed 1994, respectively, all Wallsend). This trio of the new Type 23 Duke Class frigates was ordered by the Admiralty in late 1989. They are designed primarily for anti-submarine warfare. Their diesel electric engines allow them to run at very low speeds while powerful sonars scan the ocean depths for submarines over a wide area. These frigates are highly automated and therefore have a small crew of only 160. Weapons carried include missile systems, a 115mm shore bombardment gun and helicopter armaments. The first to be delivered was HMS *Westminster*, which had been launched in February 1992.

HMS *Northumberland*

Northumberland entered the Tyne two months after her sister, *Westminster*. Fittingly, the launch was carried out by the Duke of Northumberland. Many local organisations within the county became affiliated to the ship, including the county council and Northumberland Rugby Union, which presented her with pennants to be flown on special occasions.

*The penultimate frigate, HMS **Northumberland** on her Wallsend berth prior to launch.*

*HMS **Richmond** leaves for delivery on November 3 1994.*

HMS *Richmond*

The final Type 23 sister, *Richmond*, was launched in April 1993. What may be the last ship built on the Tyne departed the river for delivery on 3 November 1994. It was a sad moment when HMS *Richmond* slipped away from Swan's jetty at Wallsend to the strains of *Now is the Hour*, played by the shipyard band.

As she moved down river thousands lined the banks in silence as if watching a funeral cortege. A sense of loss, bewilderment, disbelief and anger swept the community. But as with the many ships that had gone before, HMS *Richmond* had been built with pride.

Other major ships built, fitted out or refitted on the Tyne, and at Haverton Hill on the Tees.

Esso Northumbria (Yard No. 3, Wallsend, completed 1970). The first of eight supertankers built at Wallsend between 1968 and 1976. *Esso Northumbria* left the Tyne on her delivery voyage on 8 February 1970. The ship was 1,143 ft long and 170 ft wide – a true ocean giant. On each voyage from the Persian Gulf to Britain she could carry 70 million gallons of oil. A world slump in oil prices cut short her career after only 13 years and she went to the breaker's yard in Taiwan in 1983.

Grey Rover (Yard No. 7, Hebburn, completed 1970). Like her two sisters, *Green Rover* and *Blue Rover*, this fleet tanker cost around £3 million to build. *Grey Rover* was commissioned in April 1970. However, serious design problems meant that all three ships had to have their main engines replaced in 1973 by Smiths Dock at North Shields. In recent years she has been a support ship on Royal Navy deployments to the Falklands. In January 1994 she took part in the first Royal Navy visit to Cape Town, South Africa, for 27 years.

Blue Rover (Yard No. 8, Hebburn, completed 1970). This tanker has seen service in several world troublespots in support of the Royal Navy. In 1976 she was involved in Cod War operations off Iceland and in 1982 gained battle honours in the Falklands campaign. She has also served in support of the Armilla Patrol in the Persian Gulf. In 1993 *Blue Rover* was sold to the Portuguese Navy who renamed her *Berrio*. She is still in service.

Tabaristan (Yard No. 9, Readhead's, completed 1970). Launched in January 1969, *Tabaristan* was one of a long list of ships built by the yard for the Strick Line. Their vessels ran on services from British and European ports to the Persian Gulf. *Tabaristan* was delivered seven weeks ahead of schedule. She was fitted with a 150-ton capacity derrick for heavy lift work. In 1972 she was transferred within the P & O Group and renamed *Stratharlick*. This ship was sold to Greek owners in 1978. She went to the breaker's yard in India in 1986.

Vortigern (Yard No. 10, Neptune, completed 1969). One of several ferries to be built at Neptune, Vortigern was a combined roll on/roll off car and train ferry. She was capable of carrying 1,000 passengers on British Rail's routes between the UK and near-Continental ports. In 1982 the ship received considerable bottom damage when she hit a sea wall at the entrance to Ostend harbour in thick fog. Later she served on British Rail's Holyhead-Dun Laoghaire run across the Irish Sea. In April 1988 she was sold to Greek operators, renamed *Milos Express* and placed on services to the Greek Cyclades Islands.

Faraday (Yard No. 12, Hebburn, completed 1971). A large liquefied gas carrier built for the Nile Steamship Co. Ltd. and chartered out to an Anglo-French consortium, Ocean Gas Transport Ltd., *Faraday* traded worldwide for 23 years before being broken up in China.

Dart America (Yard No. 14, Walker, completed 1970). The first fully containerised carrying ship to be built by Swan's, she was one of the largest of her type at the time of completion. *Dart America* was launched by Princess Alexandra in May 1970. The vessel was constructed to carry over 1,500 containers on a run from Antwerp and Southampton across the Atlantic to Halifax, Nova Scotia and New York. In September 1971 she suffered a serious engine breakdown and drifted in the Atlantic for four days. Eventually a salvage tug reached her and towed her into Southampton. Later she was renamed *Manchester Challenge* and by 1988 had been renamed yet again, this time sailing as the *OOCL Challenge* when operating for Far East owner CY Tung.

Amra (Yard No. 16, Readhead's, completed 1969). The first of a pair of heavy lift ships constructed for the British India Line, *Amra* was fitted with a 200-ton derrick for the line's service between Japan and the Persian Gulf. In June 1975 she was at anchor in Kobe harbour, Japan, waiting to discharge her cargo when she was hit by a Norwegian tanker. *Amra* suffered extensive damage, but was eventually repaired and returned to service. In 1979 she was sold to the Hyundai Corporation and renamed *Halla Pride*. In October of that year *Halla Pride* went aground in the outer harbour of Busan, South Korea, sustaining heavy damage. However, the ship was repaired and continued to trade for another five years before being broken up.

Aska (Yard No. 17, Readhead's, completed 1970). Built for the same service as her sister, *Amra*, she was also sold to Hyundai, being renamed *Halla Pilot* in 1979. After a useful but uneventful career the ship was broken up in South Korea in April 1985.

Matadi Palm (Yard No. 20, Furness, completed 1970). An oil products tanker built for Unilever Brothers' shipping division Palm Line, she was to have been constructed at Hebburn but was transferred to the Tees yard. Her main route was from West Africa to European ports carrying palm oil and similar cargoes. In 1985 she was sold to Cypriot owners and renamed *Modesty*.

Manora (Yard No. 21, Neptune, completed 1970). One of four cargo ships built for the British India Line. In the mid 1970s *Manora* was transferred with her sisters to the P & O general cargo division and renamed *Strathmay*. Reorganisation within the P & O Group led to the sale of the sisters in 1982 to the United Thai Shipping Corporation who renamed her *Jumpa*. She served with them until broken up in 1988.

Morvada (Yard No. 23, Neptune, completed 1971). This ship took 17 months to construct and achieved over 21 knots on trials in July 1971. P & O renamed her *Strathmore* and then *Thais Intanin*. She went to the breaker's yard in 1986.

Mulbera (Yard No. 24, Neptune, completed 1971). The final ship of the quartet, she ran trials in December 1971. By 1982 she was owned by a Bermudan company who renamed her the *Sonia M*. She sailed on the shipping lanes of Central America for nine years and then was sold to Maltese owners who kept her for a year before she was sent to India for breaking up.

London Lion (Yard No. 29, Wallsend, completed 1972). The first of a pair of supertankers built for a subsidiary of an American corporation, *London Lion* was transferred within this corporation to the Liberian flag in 1978 and was renamed *Tropical Lion*. In April 1981 the ship became a storage vessel at Arzanah Island in the Persian Gulf. A floating mine damaged her in 1989 while she was trans-shipping oil to a British tanker and 10,000 barrels of oil escaped into the Gulf.

Four oil-bulk-ore (OBO) carriers were launched at the Swan Hunter-owned Haverton Hill Yard on the Tees between 1970 and 1975. These ships were designed to carry 167,000 tonnes of cargo. They were:

Furness Bridge (Yard No. 25, Furness, completed 1971). This vessel shipped coal or iron ore from the USA to Japan and oil from the Persian Gulf to Europe. *Furness Bridge* was launched by the Duchess of Kent in October 1970. Between 1977 and 1986 she sailed under four different owners, finishing her days as the *Ocean Sovereign*. The ship was broken up in China in March 1992.

Tyne Bridge (Yard No. 26, Furness, completed 1972). Completed in April 1972, *Tyne Bridge* was damaged by an engine room fire off Valparaiso, Chile, the following year. A year later came another mishap. The ship had to make a run for the open sea when a severe typhoon hit her discharging port. She also suffered another engine room fire but was repaired at Yokohama, Japan. Later she sailed for Italian and Taiwanese owners before being broken up in Taiwan in 1987.

English Bridge (Yard No. 27, Furness, completed 1973). Like her earlier sisters, she was built for the Seabridge Consortium, construction costs amounting to nearly £7 million. *English Bridge* was sold in 1979 to Liberian interests. By 1985 she had experienced three more changes of name and owners. Her final name was the *Kowloon Bridge*. On 22 November 1986 the ship was on passage from Canada to Scotland with iron ore when she ran into serious trouble in heavy seas. The crew were airlifted off the ship while she was southwest of Ireland. The drifting *Kowloon Bridge* was doomed and the next day she hit the Stag Rocks off the Irish coast, causing a major oil pollution problem from her 20,000 tonnes of heavy fuel oil bunkers.

Sir John Hunter (Yard No. 31, Furness, completed 1974). This oil-bulk-ore carrier (OBO) was built for a Norwegian-British consortium. In her first year of operation the *Sir John Hunter* shipped 416,000 tons of oil and 425,000 tons of iron ore worldwide. By 1991 she had changed ownership six times. Her latest name for Cypriot owners is *Nafsika M*.

Liverpool Bridge (Yard No. 57, Furness, completed 1976). The final sister in this class of OBO carriers, *Liverpool Bridge* was launched on 5 December 1975. She was built for the Bibby Line of Liverpool. Tragedy struck the following year when an explosion in her auxiliary boiler room caused the death of one of her crew while she was at anchor off Flushing in the Netherlands. The ship was repaired and returned to service. In 1978 she was renamed *Derbyshire* by her owners and it was under this name that she met disaster in September 1980 while sailing off Japan during the typhoon season. The *Derbyshire* sank with the loss of all aboard. The reason for the ship's loss is still the subject of intense debate and controversy. Allegations of structural weakness have been made and the wreck has been located in sections. It is to be hoped that the mystery surrounding the tragedy will be solved for the sake of the relatives of those who died.

Lincolnshire (Yard No. 34, Hebburn, completed 1972). A liquefied gas carrier, she was delivered to the Bibby Line of Liverpool in 1972. She has traded successfully but uneventfully, pursuing her trade around the oceans of the world.

Stolt Lion (Yard No. 35, Hebburn, completed 1971). A highly sophisticated ship designed to carry separately but at the same time a wide range of chemicals and petroleum products. She was the first ship to be built for the Anglomar Shipping Company and was chartered out for 10 years to the Norwegian Stolt Nielsen Group. *Stolt Lion* was then sold to Indian owners who ran her as the *Pavan Doot*. Sold in 1989 to Greek owners, she became *Kydon* and traded in South American waters.

Sheaf Field (Yard No. 37, Readhead's, completed 1971). A general tramp ship, she was constructed for the Sheaf Steamship Co. (W.A. Souter, Newcastle). By 1987 the vessel was sailing under the name *Fidelity* and was owned by the Kirin Shipping Co. of Cyprus. However, her career with them was cut short. In January 1988 she arrived in Durban, South Africa, with major engine trouble, encountered while on passage between Ghana and Japan. Repairs were considered too expensive and she was sent to the breaker's yard.

Chemical Venturer (Yard No. 38, Hebburn, completed 1972). Like her sister, *Chemical Explorer*, the *Chemical Venturer* ran upon the world's sea lanes with oil and chemical products. In 1986 she was sold and renamed *Venturer*. She then traded along the West African coast in tandem with her sister.

Rumuera (Yard No. 40, Walker, completed 1973). At the time of her completion in 1973 *Rumuera* was the world's largest and fastest refrigerated container ship. She was built to operate a service between Europe and New Zealand, being assigned to the P & O sector of a British consortium of shipowners. This successful container vessel is still in service. In 1977 she took the name *Rumuera Bay* and in 1993 became *Berlin Express*.

Zaida (Yard No. 44, Readhead's, completed 1972). Along with her sister, *Zira*, she was constructed to operate a service between New Zealand and Japan, carrying cargo in refrigerated chambers as well as containers. In 1972 *Zaida* rescued 17 Taiwanese fishermen who had been shipwrecked on a reef near New Caledonia in the Pacific. The ship was lengthened in Genoa, Italy, in 1979 and sold to the Ofer Brothers of Israel in 1986. She was renamed the *Avocado Carmel* and placed on services carrying citrus fruits and other cargoes from Israel.

Zira (Yard No. 45, Readhead's, completed 1972). *Zira* had the distinction of being the last ship to be built for the British India Line, one of the pillars of the British mercantile fleet. Her career mirrored that of her sister, *Zaida*. *Zira* was also lengthened in Italy and sold to the same Israeli owners. She took the name *Galia Carmel* and is still in service.

Joseph R. Smallwood (Yard No. 46, Hebburn, completed 1972). The first of two oil products tankers constructed for Common Brothers of Newcastle, she was built with a long-term charter arranged to trans-ship aviation fuel from Newfoundland in Canada to major airports of the north-eastern USA and Canada. By 1981 she had been sold to Greek owners who ran her for 10 years then sold her to Italians as the *Polare*.

Frank D. Moores (Yard No. 47, Hebburn, completed 1973). This ship had the misfortune to break in two in the Cabot Strait off Newfoundland in March 1979 after her hull was severely fractured by ice floes. The ship's aft section was saved and towed to Amsterdam where a new forward section was built. She emerged from the dockyard with a new name, the *Simonburn*. The ship was sold to Chinese interests for a spell before she passed into Greek ownership, sailing under the name *Sea Bravery*.

Capulet (Yard No. 48, Furness, completed 1973). A tramping bulk carrier built for the Bowring Steamship Co. Ltd. She traded worldwide, carrying almost 26,000 tonnes of cargo. *Capulet* was sold to Russian interests in 1984 and is still sailing, having taken the name *Yargara*.

Meadowbank (Yard No. 50, Wallsend, completed 1973). This vessel was one of six ordered for Bank Line's round-the-world service. The only ship of the class to be built at Wallsend, *Meadowbank* served with the Bank Line for 14 years, including a period of charter. She was then sold to Cypriot owners for a service between Brazil and Japan. The vessel was renamed *Pro Atlantica*.

Moraybank (Yard No. 51, Readhead's, completed 1973). *Moraybank* still maintains her round-the-world service 22 years after completion at the South Shields yard.

Forthbank (Yard No. 52, Hebburn, completed 1973). *Forthbank* and her sisters were built with large vegetable oil tanks capable of carrying 29,000 tonnes back to Europe from the Pacific. She is still in service.

Clydebank (Yard No. 53, Hebburn, completed 1974). This ship had an unlucky start to her career when a large section of her bottom was damaged while she was running trials off the Farne Islands. Repairs took several months. In 1984 she was delayed for five days by Greenpeace protesters while berthed at Darwin, Australia, to load uranium for Germany. *Clydebank* is still in service.

Ivybank (Yard No. 54, Readhead's, completed 1974). The final ship of the £20 million order, *Ivybank* was completed in June 1974. She too is still sailing.

Sir Alexander Glen (Yard No. 55, Furness, completed 1975). Completed for the Thornhope Shipping Company, the *Sir Alexander Glen* was an oil-bulk-ore (OBO) carrier. She traded throughout the world and was sold several times. Her final days were spent with Taiwanese owners under the name *Ocean Mandarin*. She was broken up in China in 1992.

Alnwick Castle (Yard No. 56, Walker, completed 1974). Built for the Bamburgh Shipping Co. Ltd. (W.A. Souter, Newcastle), *Alnwick Castle* was launched by the Duchess of Northumberland. This bulk carrier of 108,000 deadweight tonnes was completed in 1974. She was placed on a seven year charter to the Australian National Line and used for taking iron ore from Mount Newman, Western Australia, to the Port Kembla steelworks in New South Wales. Later she served with two British shipping companies, the Ben and Graig lines before being sold in 1993 to the Staccato Marine Co. Ltd. and renamed *Ariana*. She is still in service.

Windsor Lion (Yard No. 58, Wallsend, completed 1975). One of Wallsend's eight supertankers. *Windsor Lion*, like her sister *London Lion*, was built for a subsidiary of an American corporation and has traded on the world's oil routes. She was sold in 1988 to the Iranian Tanker Company and renamed *Avaj 2*. The ship is still in service.

Gold Rover (Yard No. 59, Neptune, completed 1974). A fleet replenishment tanker designed to support Royal Navy warships on long-range deployments. *Gold Rover* is still in service.

Black Rover (Yard No. 60, Neptune, completed 1974). Another tanker serving with the Royal Fleet Auxiliary Service, *Black Rover* took part in a round-the-world Royal Navy voyage in 1979. This was followed by tours of duty in the West Indies, Falkland Islands and the Persian Gulf. During the Turkish invasion of Cyprus in 1974 the ship evacuated tourists to safety. She is still in service.

HMS Glasgow (Yard No. 62, Neptune, completed 1979). This ship holds sad memories for ex-workers at Neptune. Eight of their colleagues died as a result of a fire on board while she was fitting out in September 1976. A sister to *Newcastle*, the *Glasgow* was commissioned in 1979. Two years later she was slightly damaged in a minor accident involving a Russian cruiser off northern Norway. *Glasgow* had been shadowing Russian fleet exercises. During the Falklands War the ship was holed by an Argentine bomb which passed through the auxiliary engine room. Despite the damage she managed to limp back to Britain and was repaired. *Glasgow* has since been employed on NATO duties and on the Armilla patrol in the Persian Gulf. She is still in service.

Everett F. Wells (Yard No. 64, Wallsend, completed 1977). She was the last supertanker to be launched at Wallsend and was completed in 1977 for the Ashland Oil Co. Ltd, an American operator. Sold several times, the depressed state of the oil market brought an early end to her career and she was broken up in Taiwan in 1986. Her final name was *Guam*.

Kara Lynn (Yard No. 66, Hebburn and Walker, completed 1976). This ship and her sisters, *Interoceanic I* and *Interoceanic II*, were of the same class of tanker as the *Yorkshire*. Although nominally owned by Nikreis Maritime (Cayman) Co Ltd, they came under the overall control of the Robin International Corporation which organised trade between the West and the Soviet Union during the years of the Cold War. One of the deals was to supply a number of tankers to the Soviet Union. Built in two sections like the *Yorkshire*, *Kara Lynn* was joined together at Hebburn Dock in December 1975. This ship and her sisters were part of a bizarre wedding gift that Christina Onassis gave to her Russian husband, a shipping expert, in 1979. The tankers lasted longer than the marriage! *Kara Lynn* was later renamed *Olympic Splendour*. In 1984 she rescued 37 Vietnamese boat people in the South China Sea. *Olympic Splendour* is still in service.

Interoceanic I (Yard No. 67, Furness, completed 1977). Originally scheduled for construction on the Tyne, this tanker was transferred to the Tees. Built for the Nikreis Maritime, she took her Russian name, *Geroi Novorossiyska*, shortly after delivery. Bought in the 1979 Onassis deal, she still sails under Greek ownership as the *Artemis Garofalidis*.

Interoceanic II (Yard No. 68, Furness, completed 1978). Her career mirrors that of her sister, *Interoceanic I*, and she is still in service, sailing for Liberian owners under the name *Equator*. Her Russian name was *Geroi Kerchi*.

Lagoven Santa Rita and **Lagoven Quiriquire** (Yard Nos. 78 and 79, Hebburn, both completed 1978). These two oil products tankers of 30,000 tonnes were also built under the Swan Maritime deal and sold to the Venezuelan state oil company Lagoven. Built at a cost of around £7 million each, the ships are used as shuttle tankers in and around the oil fields and export points of Venezuela.

Trinculo (Yard No. 80, Hebburn Dock, completed 1978). A bulk carrier with a cargo capacity of 29,000 tonnes, she was built for the Bowring Steamship Co. Ltd. and designed for general tramping duties. Several owners have run her since she was first sold in 1984. She currently operates under the name *Sumadija*. The ship's Sulzer engines give her a service speed of 15 knots.

Gandara (Yard No. 83, Hebburn, completed 1976). The ship was the last liquefied gas carrier to be built at Hebburn. Constructed for P & O, she has a tank capacity of 22,711 cubic metres of liquefied gas. P & O sold all their gas tanker fleet in 1986 to the Norwegian Kvaerner Group for whom she still operates as the *Helikon*.

Begonia (Yard No. 88, Walker, completed 1978). This bulk carrier was constructed along similar lines to the *Trinculo*. *Begonia* was the last ship to be built for the North Shields tramp ship company Stag Line. She was completed in 1978 and sold after seven years of trading for the line. The vessel currently trades worldwide as the *Jennifer Jane* under the Cypriot flag.

Desdemona (Yard No. 89, Hebburn, completed 1978). A sister to *Trinculo*, she was also ordered by the Bowring Steamship Co. Ltd. The ship was the last to be constructed for the company before they withdrew from shipping and concentrated on other interests. In 1984 she was sold to Yugoslav owners. Later she passed into Panamanian ownership and now sails as the *Achilles*, tramping the globe in the bulk cargo trades.

Strait of Canso (Yard No. 90, Readhead's, completed 1975). The third ship in a quartet of oil products tankers built for Common Brothers subsidiaries. She passed through the hands of several owners before ending up under Communist Chinese ownership as the *Xiang Hai*.

Hindustan (Yard No. 91, Readhead's, completed 1976). This vessel was launched unnamed from the South Shields yard in May 1976 because the Canadian oil charter work for which she was intended had fallen through. However, the tanker was bought by a New Zealand company in 1979 and spent the next 14 years shuttling oil products around the New Zealand coast. *Hindustan* was sold to Cypriots in 1993.

Kharg (Yard No. 98, Walker, completed 1985). In the early 1970s the Shah of Iran had the dream of making his country the greatest sea power in the Indian Ocean. To this end his government embarked on a large building programme. The only ship of the fleet built on the Tyne was the *Kharg*, a large refuelling tanker based on the British Royal Fleet Auxiliary 'Olna' class of oilers. She was completed in 1980, but stayed at the Walker jetty for five years awaiting the outcome of the convulsions which were racking the Middle East at the time. The Iraq-Iran War was going on and American hostages were held in Iran following the country's revolution. However, *Kharg* was eventually delivered to the country for which she had been intended and is currently the largest vessel in the Iranian Navy.

Singularity (Yard No. 594, Readhead's, completed 1977). This small cargo vessel was the last ship to be built at the Readhead's yard in South Shields and the contract was numbered so that she became the last in the sequence of Readhead-numbered vessels. Launched on 17 March 1976, *Singularity* was constructed for F.T. Everard. In 1983 she made two trips to the Falklands with supplies for the garrison there. The ship 'tramped' to many other parts of the world before being sold in 1987 to Italian owners who renamed her *Singolarita*. She is still in service.

Aldrington (Yard No. 340, Neptune, completed 1978). This small bulk carrier was to have been built at the Cleland's yard at Willington Quay but was transferred to Neptune – hence the unusual yard number. She was built for Stephenson Clarke Shipping to carry coal down the East Coast to the power stations of the South. In January 1980 a serious fire on board disabled her off the Essex coast and she was towed to Tilbury Power Station. The damage caused by the blaze meant the ship had to be given a new engine. *Aldrington* was later transferred from coal to more varied cargo carrying.

Copenhagen (Yard No. 1085, Neptune, completed 1974). A passenger vessel, *Copenhagen* was one of four ships ordered from Vickers at Barrow in 1969 by a Danish consortium. She was designed to operate a cruise service off the US West Coast. However, financial problems arose while she was still on the stocks at Barrow, which meant her building was suspended. Later a compromise was reached and Vickers sub-contracted Swan Hunter to finish the ship. She was towed to the Tyne in April 1973 and completed at the Neptune yard. Afterwards, she returned to Barrow while negotiations continued over the financial arrangements. The outcome was that the *Copenhagen* was sold to Russia, initially sailing as the *Odessa* on a worldwide cruise service, the ship having accommodation for 570.

HMS Cardiff (Yard No. 1091, Hebburn, completed 1979). Vickers at Barrow were so busy with work that they turned to Swans to help them complete this Type 42 destroyer. Accordingly, *Cardiff* was towed into the Tyne in February 1976. Commissioned in September 1979, the ship served with distinction during the Falklands conflict. She has also had several tours of duty in the West Indies helping in anti-drug smuggling operations. *Cardiff* won battle honours during the Gulf War, her helicopter being involved with the sinking of 10 Iraqi gunboats. In more recent times the ship has carried out embargo duties in the Adriatic.

Crown Prince (Yard No. 104, Walker, completed 1979). The first of two small container ships built for the Furness Withy organisation to run on routes between Britain and the eastern Mediterranean, *Crown Prince* was sold in 1985 to Thai owners and now operates a shuttle service between Bangkok and Hong Kong.

Royal Prince (Yard No. 105, Walker, completed 1982). This ship, and her sister *Crown Prince*, were to have been launched on the same day, but gales upset the plans. The career of *Royal Prince* has mirrored that of her sister. However, she has had one moment of fame. During the war in Lebanon in 1982 she helped to evacuate several hundred Britons from the country, ferrying them from the Lebanese port of Jounieh to the safety of Larnaca in Cyprus. Like her sister, she was sold in 1985 and has traded in the Far East ever since.

Dunedin (Yard No. 107, Walker, completed 1980). Dunedin was part of a joint venture by British owners in the refrigerated container trade to New Zealand. Built for the once famous Shaw Savill and Albion Line, she sailed between New Orleans and New Zealand via ports of call in the Caribbean. The vessel was sold in 1986 to German owners who had her lengthened. *Dunedin* then traded to South America, being renamed *Monte Pascoal*. In 1990 she was switched to a trans-Pacific service for another owner and now runs under the name *Columbus Olivos*.

HMS York (Yard No. 111, Neptune, completed 1985). A stretched version of the Type 42 destroyer, *York* was deployed shortly after her commissioning to the Far East. Her assignment was to act as guardship for the Royal Yacht *Britannia* during the Queen's visit to Hong Kong and China. The *York* paid a six-day visit to Shanghai, the first British warship to do so for many decades. Since then she has been a typical workhorse of the fleet, with tours of duty in the Falklands, Mediterranean and the Persian Gulf.

Ingram Osprey (Yard No. 114, Neptune, completed 1982). This oil products tanker has a cargo capacity of 30,000 tonnes and was built for the Ingram Tankships Company. While fitting out she was chartered to OSCO and took those initials as a prefix to her name, becoming *OSCO Ingram Osprey*. In 1987 she was sold to Indian owners and currently operates on routes around the Indian sub-continent's coastline.

Thorseggen (Yard No. 117, Wallsend, completed 1983). Constructed for Norwegian owners Thor Dahl, this ship was placed on a 12-year charter to transport newsprint, timber and containers down the western seaboard of Canada and the USA. *Thorseggen*'s profile is dominated by two self-discharging travelling cranes which serve all her hatches.

Atlantic Conveyor (Yard No. 121, Wallsend, completed 1985). The second ship to be named *Atlantic Conveyor*, she replaced her tragic predecessor which was sunk during the Falklands War. Also constructed for Atlantic Container Lines, this large roll on/roll off container ship can be called upon by the government in time of national emergency. To this end, the new *Atlantic Conveyor* was designed to have a detachable flight deck for helicopters which rests on top of the container guides. Today she still trades on the Atlantic shipping lanes between the USA and Europe. In 1987 she was lengthened at the Trafalgar House yard on the Clyde and can now carry over 2,700 containers.

HMS Marlborough (Yard No 127, Wallsend, completed 1991). The first of the new class of Type 23 anti-submarine frigates to be built on the Tyne. The Type 23s are more commonly known as the Duke Class frigates. *Marlborough* almost suffered a major accident during Anglo-French exercises in the Channel shortly after handover. Only luck prevented disaster when a helicopter nearly hit the ship's hangar.

GNS Yogaga, GNS Dzata (Yard No 130 Wallsend and Yard No 131, Neptune, completed 1989). These were two small fast patrol craft of the Ghanaian Navy which came to the Tyne for a major refit. They arrived in March 1988 and left the river 14 months later.

HMS Southampton (Yard No 133, Hebburn Dock, completed 1991). *Southampton* suffered major damage when she was in collision with a merchant ship during a tour of duty on the Armilla Patrol in the Persian Gulf. She arrived off the Tyne in August 1989 after being brought from Portsmouth in 'piggy-back' fashion on the dock ship *Super Servant I*. The repairs and refit took 21 months. *Southampton* sailed from the Tyne in May 1991.

RFA Fort Grange (Yard No 134, Wallsend, completed 1991). This vessel was berthed at Wallsend for three months for a major refit. She is a large replenishment ship.

*The last order. The Shields ferry **Pride of the Tyne** passes through the Swing Bridge between Newcastle and Gateshead.*

Tyne & Wear Passenger Transport Executive

Pride of the Tyne

(Yard No 140, Wallsend, completed 1993). This small passenger ferry was built for the North Shields-South Shields crossing. Ordered by the Tyne and Wear Passenger Transport Executive, she was lifted into the Tyne by one of Swan's large cranes in June 1993. As well as operating on the busy Shields ferry service across the Tyne, she also undertakes pleasure trips under charter. *Pride of the Tyne* was the first ferry incorporating all the new safety features recommended after the *Marchioness* disaster on the Thames. The little ship can now be seen regularly operating on the river of her birth. The order was the last contract to be placed with Swan Hunter. By coincidence, the first vessel built by Wigham Richardson's Neptune Yard in 1860 had also been a ferry, the *Victoria*. She ran on a service between the Isle of Wight and the mainland. Wigham Richardson's was the first constituent firm of Swan Hunter to be founded.

Vessels built, fitted out or refitted in Swan Hunter Shipbuilders Shipyards

Yard No.	Name of vessel	Owners	Keel Laid	Launch	Trials	Handover
1. Walker	Atlantic Causeway	Cunard SS Co. (ACL)	17/04/68	02/04/69	11/67	26/11/69
2. Walker	Atlantic Conveyor	Cunard SS Co. (ACL)	21/05/68	25/8/69	03/70	25/03/70
3. Wallsend	Esso Northumbria	Esso Petroleum	16/04/68	02/05/69	02/70	14/05/70
4. Wallsend	Esso Hibernia	Esso Petroleum	05/05/69	06/04/70	12/70	14/05/70
5. Wallsend	Texaco Great Britain	Texaco OT Ltd.	09/04/70	26/01/71	11-12/71	17/12/71
6. Hebburn Shipyard	Green Rover	MoD (N) RFA	04/03/68	19/12/68	7/69	15/08/69
7. Hebburn Shipyard	Grey Rover	MoD (N) RFA	04/03/68	17/04/69	3-4/70	10/04/70
8. Hebburn Shipyard	Blue Rover	MoD (N) RFA	30/01/69	11/11/69	6-7/70	15/07/70
9. South Shields	Tabaristan	Strick Line	23/05/68	17/01/69	5/69	11/05/70
10. Neptune	Vortigern	British Railways	24/07/68	05/03/69	7/69	18/07/69
11. Hebburn Shipyard	Emiliano Zapata	Petroleos Mexicanos	12/10/68	04/07/69	1-2/70	18/03/70
12. Hebburn Shipyard	Faraday	Nile Steamship Co. Ltd.)	14/04/69	19/06/70	11-12/70	04/01/71
13. Not allocated						
14. Walker	Dart America	Tynedale S. Co. (Dart Line)	15/04/69	05/05/70	11/70	11/70
15. Walker	Dart Atlantic	Bristol City Line (Dart Line)	09/11/69	14/10/70	05/71	05/71
16. South Shields	Amra	British India Nav. Co. Ltd.	19/12/68	30/06/69	11/69	15/11/69
17. South Shields	Aska	British India Nav. Co. Ltd.	22/04/69	09/01/70	05/70	21/5/70
18. Haverton Hill	Dunstanburgh Castle	Bamburgh Shipping Co.	20/01/69	25/09/69	03/70	16/03/70
19. Not allocated						
20. Haverton Hill	Matadi Palm	Palm Line Ltd.	08/10/69	20/07/70	12/70	14/12/70
21. Neptune	Manora	British India Nav. Co. Ltd.	08/07/69	21/03/70	09/70	15/09/70
22. Neptune	Merkara	British India Nav. Co. Ltd.	27/08/69	22/06/70	3/71	10/03/71
23. Neptune	Morvada	British India Nav. Co. Ltd.	11/03/70	30/11/70	7/71	23/07/71
24. Neptune	Mulbera	British India Nav. Co. Ltd.	02/07/70	14/04/71	12/71	24/12/71
25. Haverton Hill	Furness Bridge	Furness Withy Co. Ltd.	29/09/69	16/10/70	5-8/71	09/08/71
26. Haverton Hill	Tyne Bridge	Nile Steamship Co.	22/10/70	02/11/71	3-4/72	19/04/72
27. Haverton Hill	English Bridge	Bibby Line	04/11/71	25/09/72	2-3/73	06/03/73
28. Wallsend	World Unicorn	World-Wide Shipping Co.	20/03/72	03/05/73	1-2/74	13/02/74
29. Wallsend	London Lion	Anglomar Shipping	27/03/71	17/03/72	9/72	12/10/72
30. Not allocated						
31. Haverton Hill	Sir John Hunter	Thornhope Shipping Co. Ltd	29/09/72	28/08/73	01/74	24/01/74
32. South Shields	Nigaristan	Strick Line	14/11/69	04/06/70	10/70	29/10/70
33. Walker	Rangatira	Union SS Co. Ltd.	02/04/70	23/06/71	12/71	13/01/72
34. Hebburn	Lincolnshire	Bibby Line	30/06/70	12/07/71	12/71	09/03/72
35. Hebburn	Stolt Lion	Anglomar Shipping	02/02/70	15/10/70	07/71	14/07/71
36. Hebburn Shipyard	Chemical Explorer	Anglo Eastern Bulk	26/10/70	20/10/71	04/72	04/05/72
37. South Shields	Sheaf Field	Sheaf SS Co.	31/05/70	11/11/70	03/71	17/03/71
38. Hebburn Shipyard	Chemical Venturer	Anglo Eastern Bulk	19/05/71	16/03/72	08/72	04/09/72
39. Neptune	Vistafjord	Norweg. Amer. Line	19/04/71	15/05/72	04/73	15/05/73
40. Walker	Rumuera	P & O (Overseas Container Lines)	07/01/71	12/06/72	9-12/73	13/12/73
41. Walker	Cancelled	Shaw Savill (Overseas Container Lines)				
42. Wallsend	Cancelled	Blue Star (Overseas Container Lines)				
43. Wallsend	Cancelled	Port Line (Overseas Container Lines)				
44. South Shields	Zaida	British India Nav. Co. Ltd.	02/10/70	24/06/71	12/71	07/01/72
45. South Shields	Zira	British India Nav. Co. Ltd.	08/04/71	01/02/72	06/72	09/11/72

Yard No.	Name of vessel	Owners	Keel Laid	Launch	Trials	Handover
46. Hebburn Shipyard	Joseph R. Smallwood	Nile Steamship Co. Ltd.	22/10/71	11/07/72	12/72	21/12/72
47. Hebburn Shipyard	Frank D. Moores	Nile Steamship Co. Ltd.	07/04/72	06/02/73	06/73	19/06/73
48. Haverton Hill	Capulet	Bowring Steamship Co.	29/10/70	29/03/72	06/72	16/06/73
49. South Shields	Corabank	Bank Line	29/11/71	25/08/72	02/73	23/03/73
50. Wallsend	Meadowbank	Bank Line	02/02/72	21/11/72	03/73	23/03/73
51. South Shields	Moraybank	Bank Line	30/05/72	01/06/73	11/73	16/11/73
52. Hebburn Shipyard	Forthbank	Bank Line	29/07/72	31/05/73	10/73	8/11/73
53. Hebburn Shipyard	Clydebank	Bank Line	02/02/73	26/11/73	07/74	18/07/74
54. South Shields	Ivybank	Bank Line	14/12/72	07/02/74	06/74	06/74
55. Haverton Hill	Sir Alexander Glen	Thornhope Shipping Co. Ltd.	30/08/73	14/11/74	3/75	04/75
56. Walker	Alnwick Castle	Bamburgh Shipping Co.	15/06/72	14/09/73	04/74	18/04/74
57. Haverton Hill	Liverpool Bridge	Bibby Line	17/11/74	05/12/75	05/76	10/06/76
58. Wallsend	Windsor Lion	Anglomar Shipping	04/05/73	21/06/74	04-5/75	13/06/75
59. Neptune	Gold Rover	MoD (N) RFA	28/02/72	07/03/73	02/74	22/03/74
60. Neptune	Black Rover	MoD (N) RFA	05/06/72	30/08/73	07-08/74	23/08/74
61. Neptune	HMS Newcastle	MoD (N) Type 42	21/02/73	24/04/75	04-05/77	25/02/78
62. Neptune	HMS Glasgow	MoD (N) Type 42	16/04/74	14/04/76		09/03/79
63. Wallsend	Tyne Pride	Meridor Tankers	24/06/74	06/10/75	10-11/76	12/11/76
64. Wallsend	Everett F. Wells	Ashland Oil Co. Ltd.	07/10/75	24/09/76		07/77
65. Hebburn Dock	Yorkshire (Fore)	Bibby Line	17/12/73		05/75	10/75
Walker	(Aft)		30/10/73	01/10/74		
66. Walker	Kara Lynn (Aft)	Nikreis Maritime (Swan Maritime) 3/10/74		04/12/75	04/76	05/76
Hebburn Dock	(Fore)					
67. Haverton Hill	Interoceanic I	Nikreis Maritime (Swan Maritime) 23/01/76		22/01/77	29/09/77	10/77
68. Haverton Hill	Interoceanic II	Nikreis Maritime (Swan Maritime) 25/02/76		7/2/77		02/78
69. Hebburn Shipyard	Helena 'K'	Nikreis Maritime (Swan Maritime) 06/07/73		04/07/74	02/75	26/02/75
70. Neptune	Robkap I	Nikreis Maritime (Swan Maritime) 07/09/73		13/11/74	05/75	
71. Hebburn Shipyard	Robkap II	Nikreis Maritime (Swan Maritime) 07/07/74		16/02/76	06/76	06/07/76
72. Neptune	Robkap III	Nikreis Maritime (Swan Maritime) 13/11/74		13/04/76	08/76	15/09/76
73. Hebburn Shipyard	Robkap IV	Nikreis Maritime (Swan Maritime) 22/10/75		08/09/76	12/76	19/12/76
74.-75. Cancelled		Gazocean (Houlder)				
76.-77. Cancelled		Swan Maritime				
78. Hebburn Shipyard	Lagoven Santa Rita	Lagoven SA Venezuela	24/02/76	02/05/77	03/78	29/03/78
79. Hebburn Shipyard	Lagoven Quiriquire	Lagoven SA Venezuela	29/10/76	12/10/77	05/78	08/06/78
80. Hebburn Dock	Trinculo	Bowring	25/01/77	06/10/77	02/78	08/02/78
81.-82. Cancelled		Swan Maritime				
83. Hebburn Shipyard	Gandara	P & O	28/11/73	20/10/75	03/76	30/03/76
84-87. Cancelled		Swan Maritime				
88. Walker	Begonia	Stag Line	15/09/76	13/07/77	05/78	25/05/78
89. Hebburn Shipyard	Desdemona	Bowring SS Co. Ltd.	17/10/77	16/05/78	06/78	11/07/78
90. South Shields	Strait of Canso	Common Bros.	18/12/73	25/04/75	10/75	27/10/75
91. South Shields	MV Hindustan	Common Bros.	29/04/75	12/05/76	09/76	24/09/76
92.-93. Cancelled		Swan Maritime				
94.-97. Not allocated						
98. Walker	IIS Kharg	Imperial Iranian Navy (oiler)	27/01/76	03/02/77	09/85	10/85
101. Neptune	HMS Exeter	MoD (N) Type 42	22/07/76	25/04/78	11-12/79	30/08/80
102. Walker	HMS Illustrious	MoD (N) Aircraft Carrier	07/10/76	01/12/78	11/81-1/82	18/06/82
103. Wallsend	Pontoon (2 parts)	Nigerian Ports Authority	12/76	17/01/77	None	01/02/77

Yard No.	Name of vessel	Owners	Keel Laid	Launch	Trials	Handover
104. Walker	Royal Prince	Furness Withy	02/11/77	16/10/78	11/81-01/82	18/06/82
105. Walker	Crown Prince	Furness Withy	11/11/77	17/10/78	09/79	17/09/79
106. Hebburn Shipyard	Pacific Swan	BNFL	14/12/77	20/07/78	12/78	26/01/79
107. Walker	Dunedin	Shaw Savill & Albion	19/02/79	15/02/80	06/80	13/07/80
108. Hebburn Dock	MS Kopalnia Gottwald	Polish Steamship Co.	02/03/79	08/11/79	01/80	25/01/80
109. Wallsend	HMS Ark Royal	MoD (N) Aircraft Carrier	14/12/78	02/06/81	10-12/84	01/07/85
110. Hebburn Dock	Pacific Crane	BNFL	02/05/79	17/03/80	07/80	14/08/80
111. Neptune	HMS York	MoD (N) Type 42 (Stretched)	18/01/80	21/6/82	8-10/84	25/03/85
112. Hebburn Dock	BP Achiever	BP Tanker Co.	05/09/80	18/03/83	05/83	12/07/83
114. Walker	Ingram Osprey	Ingram Tanker Co.	19/09/80	12/11/81	04/82	05/82
115. Hebburn Dock	Mediterranean Shearwater	BNFL	06/10/80	01/07/81	11/81	01/12/81
116. Hebburn Dock	Pacific Teal	BNFL	28/08/81	26/04/82	10-11/82	24/11/82
117. Wallsend	Thorseggen	Thor Dahl	08/01/82	16/09/82	02/83	21/07/83
118. Wallsend	Hoegh Duke	Leif Hoegh	31/08/82	06/09/83	12-16/04/84	12/06/84
119. Not allocated						
120. Neptune	Orelia (Hull only)	Houlder Offshore	06/82	11/12/82	None	18/12/82
121. Wallsend	Atlantic Conveyor	Cunard (ACL)	13/06/83	12/07/84	12/84	14/01/85
122. Neptune	Pacific Guardian	Cable & Wireless	21/07/83	13/06/84	24/10/84	11/84
123. Neptune	HMS Sheffield	MoD (N) Type 22	02/02/84	26/03/86	01-03/88	25/03/88
124. Wallsend	HMS Coventry	MoD (N) Type 22	29/03/84	08/04/86	12/87-02/88	01/07/88
125. Wallsend	RFA Sir Galahad	MoD (N) LSL	12/07/85	13/12/86	6-7/88	10/07/88
126. Neptune	HMS Chatham	MoD (N) Type 22	12/05/86	20/01/88	8-10/88	04/05/89
127. Wallsend	HMS Marlborough	MoD (N) Type 23	28/10/87	21/01/89	08/90-02/91	07/03/91
128. Wallsend	Sir Eric Sharp	Cable & Wireless	21/01/88	25/10/88	16/03/89	22/03/89
129. Wallsend	RFA Fort George	MoD (N)	09/03/89	01/03/91	01-03/93	30/03/93
130. Wallsend	Yogaga (refit)	Ghana Navy	10/03/88 (arrival)			14/06/89
131. Wallsend	Dzata (refit)	Ghana Navy	10/03/88 (arrival)			14/06/89
132. Wallsend	James Clark Ross	Nat. Env. Res. Council	23/04/90	01/12/90	08/91	25/09/91
133. Wallsend	HMS Southampton (refit)	MoD (N) Type 42	24/08/89 (arrival)		03-05/91	24/05/91
134. Wallsend	RFA Fort Grange (refit)	MoD (N) RFA	23/10/90 (arrival)			22/01/91
135. Wallsend	HMS Westminster	MOD (N) Type 23	18/01/91	04/02/92	5-7/93	19/11/93
136. Wallsend	HMS Northumberland	MoD (N) Type 23	01/04/91	04/04/92	09-11/93	24/05/94
137. Wallsend	HMS Richmond	MoD (N) Type 23	11/02/92	06/04/93	04-09/94	08/11/94
138. Neptune	IKS Arun (refit ex-Green Rover)	Indonesian Navy	15/04/92 (arrival)			12/08/92
139. Long lead items for order for new Type 23 frigate – order 'given' to Yarrows						
140. Wallsend	Pride of the Tyne	Tyne & Wear PTE	02/93	02/06/93		27/07/93
594. Readhead's	Singularity	F.T. Everard	07/07/76	17/03/77		16/06/77
1337. Neptune	Starman Anglia		10/02/77	21/07/77		10/77
340. Neptune	Aldrington	Stephenson Clarke Shipping	30/09/77	24/04/78		07/09/78
1085. Neptune	Copenhagen		01/04/73 (arrival)	20/12/72 (Barrow)		05/74
1091. Hebburn	HMS Cardiff	MoD (N) Type 42	09/02/76 (arrival)	22/02/74 (Barrow)		22/09/79
R001. Hebburn Dock	Hengist (refit)	Sealink	03/01/86 (arrival)			14/02/86
R002. Hebburn Dock	Horsa (refit)	Sealink	16/02/86 (arrival)			20/03/86

The authors regret they have been unable to include the work of Smiths Dock on the Tees and Cleland's Shipyard on the Tyne.